# PRECIOUS MEMORIES

# AND

# FUNNY - SHORT STORIES

## Of Life on the Farm

Deborah J. Rogers/Logsdon

Order this book online at www.trafford.com
or email orders@trafford.com

Most Trafford titles are also available at major online book retailers.

Note for Librarians: A cataloguing record for this book is available from Library
and Archives Canada at www.collectionscanada.ca/amicus/index-e.html

Printed in Victoria, BC, Canada.

ISBN: 978-1-4269-1508-6 (sc)

*We at Trafford believe that it is the responsibility of us all, as both individuals and corporations,
to make choices that are environmentally and socially sound. You, in turn, are supporting this
responsible conduct each time you purchase a Trafford book, or make use of our publishing services.
To find out how you are helping, please visit www.trafford.com/responsiblepublishing.html*

*Our mission is to efficiently provide the world's finest, most comprehensive book publishing
service, enabling every author to experience success. To find out how to publish your book, your
way, and have it available worldwide, visit us online at www.trafford.com*

*Trafford rev. 8/13/2009*

 www.trafford.com

**North America & international**
toll-free: 1 888 232 4444 (USA & Canada)
phone: 250 383 6864 ♦ fax: 250 383 6804 ♦ email: info@trafford.com

**The United Kingdom & Europe**
phone: +44 (0)1865 487 395 ♦ local rate: 0845 230 9601
facsimile: +44 (0)1865 481 507 ♦ email: info.uk@trafford.com

Dedicated to my family; my mother and dad, bothers, sisters, many cousins, aunts and

uncles, and especially my loving grandparents who provided me the opportunity to create

these precious memories and some funny stories.


By: Deborah J. Rogers/ Logsdon

April 15, 2009

# Introduction

For those of you who have lived on a farm or have always had a yearning to live on a farm, this book is written for you. A quick easy read that will inspire and lift your spirits. Make yourself comfortable, pour your favorite beverage and be ready to reminisce, laugh or just dream of how it must have been for farmers so many years past.

This book contains precious memories and funny short stories of a young girl growing-up on a farm in the hills of West Virginia during the 1950s' and 60s' with her mother and dad, grandparents, brothers, sisters, many cousins, aunts, and uncles. A 167 acre farm operated without fancy tractors, or gasoline powered-machinery. However there was plenty of horsepower; (4)1000 pounds of pure flesh and bones. There was no indoor plumbing, no running water, and therefore no indoor toilets. We had the privilege of owning and operating an outdoor-outhouse. There was no soft white toilet paper, only an old discarded Sears & Roebuck catalog, or the daily newspaper served the purpose. There was one crank style telephone and no elaborate electronic contraptions. One vehicle for the family's convenience; a 1950 Chevrolet pickup that only licensed drivers had access to; and used only when necessary

# The Cleanest Outhouse

Many neighbors' must have thought we had the cleanest outhouse in the holler. Each time anyone of us had to visit "The privy" we carried a broom; not to clean, but to ward-off being trapped in the privy by "Ole Tom". Time and time again we were reminded not to tease Ole Tom, but despite the warnings he was taught some bad behaviors, and became a twenty pound menace.

I was aware that everything on the farm had its purpose, and not realizing that Tom would be joining us for Thanksgiving, I decided that he needed a purpose for his life. My plan was to teach a certain shirker a lesson; I would teach Ole Tom to give them a good flogging. I began by observing Ole Tom and his reaction to certain stimulus.

To get his attention I would give out a loud gobble. His reaction; he gobbled. After several tauntings he would become extremely agitated, and come running towards me. With Tom in hot pursuit I'd raced toward the outhouse. Once inside I'd continue to gobble. Peeping through the cracks of the outhouse walls, and continually circling the outhouse, he became even more agitated as he tried to make contact with his rival. I'm sure his intention was to seek out the intruder and flog the daylights out of him.

Mission accomplished; didn't take much time he was a fast learner. Now, with Tom lurking outside it became apparent that I was trapped inside the outhouse. How will I free myself without receiving a good flogging from Ole Tom? There in the corner stood a broom; I decided this would become a mighty weapon against Tom's talons.

Through the cracks of the outhouse I watched Tom, and waited until he was behind the back wall of the outhouse. I then quickly opened the door and made a mad dash for the barnyard gate. I made it through the gate, and it slammed behind me with a loud crack! Tom came running; jumped high into the air striking the gait with his feet. Mustering all the strength I had; I began swinging the broom giving him "what for" and knocking him to the ground.

From that day forward when Ole Tom heard the barnyard gate slam he came running with every intention of attacking the person exiting the outhouse. The only means of escaping a good flogging from Ole Tom was to carry a broom with each visit. Now I'm positive that our neighbors didn't understand our predicament, and therefore believed that we must have had the cleanest outhouse in the hollow.

# Lesson Learned

As I mentioned before there was a certain shirker in our family, and each day when chores were assigned the shirker would have a sudden urge to disappear to the outhouse. Apparently the one assigning the chores had no clue as to what the shirker was doing. So, I decided to take matters into my own hands and teach the shirker a valuable lesson.

Now that I had taught Ole Tom to listen for the slamming gate, then removing the broom from the outhouse during my earlier visit, the shirker would have no means of protection from Ole Tom. After suffering just one of Tom's floggings; sharp puncturing talons, ferrous pecking of a beak and a good beating from flapping wings…. Hopefully the shirker would soon learn their lesson and gladly receive his assignment.

Our day began as usual; after having had our breakfast the seven of us kids lined-up to receive our chores for the day; the most difficult chores were assigned to the older kids, and the easier chores were left for the youngest.

After about the third assignment the shirker made a quick dash for the safety of the outhouse; thinking he would exit after the hardest chores were assigned, he sure was about to receive a frightening surprise.

I waited until the shirker made his way through the barnyard gait and the safety of the outhouse, I than began to gobble. Ole Tom was quick to respond and began trotting towards the outhouse. Standing there in line I continued to gobble; the other kids thought I had totally lost my mind and began laughing. Grandma didn't think it was funny, she believed I was "being a smart ellick", and asked "Do you think you're being cute, I suggest you stop making fun and listen-up".

The other six of us kids received our assignments. I'm certain the shirker was listening closely and knowing to whom and what the assignments were, and knowing exactly when to exit the outhouse. As we dispersed and began our daily chores, I continued to observe Ole Tom as he continued to prance around and around the outhouse, and just waiting for his moment.

Having no clue that Ole Tom was about to round the side of the outhouse next to the door, the shirker slowly opened the outhouse door then exited. As the shirker began waltzing his way towards the gate, I gave out another loud gobble. Ole Tom trotted swiftly toward the shirker, flying high into the air striking the shirker, and knocking him to the ground. The shirker let out a murderous scream that commanded everyone's attention; especially his mothers'.

As Ole Tom was teaching the shirker a good lesson, the shirkers mother picked up a set of broken toy wagon wheels and began ruthlessly beating Ole Tom, and screaming "Get off my baby!, Get off my baby!" With Tom's feathers now filling the air my aunt rendered him unconscious.

My aunt quickly picked-up her "baby", and began running towards the house. Yelling with every breath; "Who's ever responsible for this will be punished, I mean you will be severely punished!" I believe the person responsible had just received his punishment. I don't call a nine year old boy a "baby"; I call him a lazy shirker. Ole Tom taught the shirker a lesson that no human could ever teach; that shirking your duties and then having to suffer the consequences could be, and would be a very unpleasant experience; especially on this farm.

It took several more times to remind the shirker what the consequences would be if he continued his behavior; each morning thereafter as we lined-up to receive our chores for the day, the shirker needed only to hear a whispered gobble from me to remind him not to let the thought enter his mind of entering the outhouse to escape his responsibilities. The shirker stood in line and not once darted for the outhouse, I believe he finally learned a valuable lesson, one he has never forgotten.

# Not One Secret?
# Maybe

We did not receive our first "real" telephone until 1964, before such time my grandmother was the only one in the family who had a telephone. A crank-style phone; a big wooden box with a receiver an ear piece, and a hand crank; to place a call; you picked up the ear piece then placed it to your ear. With the other hand you turned the crank to dial the person of choice; one short crank for so-in-so, and two, three or four short cranks for others. For the longest time I truly believed that everyone was deaf. Each time a call was made the caller would yell into the mouth piece as if the person on the other end was deaf.

The "Real Telephone" was another type of communication contraption made of plastic, with a receiver and had a rotary dial. The most amazing part of this type of phone was that we could conduct "Unintentional Conference" calls. I believe in the business world its called Conference calls. Whereby, several people may carry-on their business transactions and discuss their plan of action.

Our unintentional conference calls began with the "Party-line". A one-line communications system that 6-8 people shared, and anyone connected to this line could simply pick-up their receiver and ease-drop on their neighbor's conversation. There were no need for business meetings; thanks to the party-line everyone knew your business.

We over heard many interesting conversations on that party-line, and there were very few secrets kept. Many feuds' began, and lots of "sweet nothings" were whispered through that contraption. If you heard a click, you best watch what you say chances were someone was listening, and the shouting began, "Get off the line!" Good piece of advice; if you felt the need to have a private conversation you best meet that person in a hayfield.

# Precious Memories
# Life Anew

After what seemed to be an endless cold winter we welcomed the sights, sounds, and the freshness of spring. Dark clouds approach and the thunder rumbles, the rain falls and the earths cleansed. The sun reappears producing a multi-colored rainbow. Our hopes are renewed as we all search for the "Pot of gold at the end of the rainbow". Our souls are rejuvenated as we run barefoot and free through the cool spring rain.

Wildflowers are now pushing their tiny heads through the warmed earth, and displaying their brightly colored faces as they reach for the life giving sun.

Birds are scurrying and gathering materials for the makings of their nests.

The swamp peepers are singing in harmony searching for the perfect mate.

The ewes are lambing and the landscape is speckled with tiny white dots.

Mares are fouling and the long legged fouls are scampering about with exuberant bursts of energy.

The "Feared" rooster struts' his stuff and crows "Cock-A-Doddle-Doo".

The hens are stretching their wings as soft clucks and peeps are heard, beneath the out stretched wings appear tiny down covered yellow chicks.

Sows are grunting and grunts are returned. The communication process between the sow and her piglets' develops. This is the farmers meaning of "Pig Latin".

The air is filled with the aromatic scent of apple and cherry blossoms.

The honey bees are busy buzzing about as they begin the long process of producing that sweet taste of natural gold.

The hayfields are alive with waist high new growth, and the grasses sway gently in the warm summer breeze. Listen closely; you can hear soft whispers from heaven. The dreary cold winter has faded, and the earth is made anew.

# The Farmer and His Team Become One

We begin to prepare the farm equipment for the work ahead; wheels are greased, blades are sharpened, and harnesses are oiled. Our horses receive their new footwear for the summer as we remove ours.

The plowing of the garden begins; the horses are harnessed with tough black leather straps, adorned with bright silver shiny buckles, and around their necks are carried heavy cotton collars. Lead straps are snapped to their bridles and harnesses.

The horses are then backed into their rightful places, side-by-side in front of the plow. Heavy pulling chains are then connected to the plow, and the command "Get-Up" is given.

The horse's heads are bobbing in unison; their tails are swishing back and forth as they trudge along at a steady gait. With metal clanging, leather squeaking, nostrils flaring and snorts expelled, the farmer gives his commands; "Gee" meaning turn right, or "Haul" meaning turn left, and at the sound of the farmer's voice the trusty beast's ears point backward to receive the commands. They obey the commands and veer either right or left. At this point the farmer and his team become one.

# A New Day Dawning

Beginning in the "wee hours of the morning" a new day is dawning and the morning ritual begins anew. Under the watchful eye of the farmer's closes companion, not his wife; the family dog! The horses are adorned once again with their appropriate attire and connected to a different piece of machinery; the mowing machine, a 700 pound hunk of metal consisting of two iron wheels, wooden single trees and traces, and a 10 foot sickle bar for mowing.

Hours pass slowly as the farmer and his team trudges along mowing acres and acres of the tall grass. Dusk approaches and the sound of the sickle bar ceases. Acres of fresh mown hay now lay strewn about the fields to bask in the warm summer sun to dry and cure. Unhitched from the machine the horses are lead back to the barn, unharnessed, groomed and turned out to pasture for a well deserved rest.

It's now time to repair or replace other pieces of equipment and tools; pitch fork handles are replaced, and long poles are gathered for the stacking of hay, hay rakes and sleds are repaired. The hay is now cured and ready to stack. All family members and neighbors' gather together for some "Fun-in the- sun", I'm not referring to the beach; the only beach the farmer visits is his hayfields.

# Need a Tromper

Let's build a haystack: First we need to obtain several 20 foot poles. A round hole is dug about six feet deep in the ground; one end of the pole is placed in the hole and secured by the dirt you just removed. The other 14 feet of the pole protrudes from the ground, and the hay is stacked around the protruding end of the pole.

Sleds are filled with huge mounds of hay and hauled to the site. Workers began pitching the hay evenly around the pole with their pitchforks. Now there's an important decision to make; who will be the "tromper"? The tromper is the person who stands near the middle of the haystack and hangs onto the pole. As the hay mound becomes higher and higher the tromper swings around the pole and compacts the hay with his/her feet, forming a nice sturdy hay stack.

The tromper is kept busy dodging the pitchforks; you can only hope that everyone can accurately gage the distance between you and their pitchfork.

# Enjoying the Ride

There's nothing more gratifying for an 8 year old than being in charge of a 1000 pound beast. Whether by means of driving the hay rake or straddling the beasts back while towing an enormous hay filled sled. Having the feeling of being in complete control of the situation is truly a confidence builder.

However there was one mare that could destroy anyone's confidence, and she usually did. On certain occasions if we were short-handed the older kids would have the unpleasant opportunity of working Old Pearl, and having good horsemanship I was usually the lucky one chosen.

Old Pearl was always flighty and a little untrustworthy. She knew the difference between adult voices and the kid's voices, therefore she knew who she could run away with and usually did. Anytime Pearl became spooked or just didn't want to work she would… in full gallop, head for the barn taking her cargo with her.

The day I lost a bit of my confidence was the day Old Pearl and I ran into a swarm of yellow jackets. The day started out as usual; I harnessed Old Pearl, backed her into the traces, hitched her to the hay rake and away we went.

We made the first pass of raking and rowing without a problem. As we were about to start the second long row, Pearl began swishing her tail frantically, stomping her huge feet and bucking wildly. I heard the bees buzzing, and before I knew what was happening Pearl began galloping at a high rate of speed; or at least as fast as her huge body would allow. I began yelling WHOA! WHOA, but she refused to heed my commands.

Hanging onto the seat of the rake for my dear life; I dropped the driving lines, loosing complete control of the situation and a bit of my confidence. The rake had no springs and no soft rubber tires to cushion my ride. Bouncing and flopping about on the seat of the rake I felt and looked just like a rag doll. She continued bucking and galloping until she reached her favorite destination; the barn.

She suffered not one sting from those yellow jackets, the sound of the buzzing bees was all the excuse she needed to bolt and run. That's a ride I'll never forget. Although I have to admit; even though I was a little frightened, and my confidence somewhat shattered, I enjoyed that ride.

# Sweat, Pain, and no "Tom Foolery"

The hay is now cured; as we begin to stack the hay the hot summer sun beats down on our snow white bodies, and there's sweat on every brow. Our skin begins to itch as the hayseed and every other weed sticks to our moist skin. From day-light-til-dark the hay is turned and rowed by the horse drawn hay rake, then pitched onto the horse drawn hay sleds. One-by-one we painstakingly erect the fourteen foot haystacks.

Dusk is fast approaching as the last haystack is stacked. We look around the meadow and see multiple stacks of large golden mounds of hay. With our sun burnt bodies, and every muscle aching, we are extremely proud of our accomplishments.

Each horse is unhitched from the sleds and rakes, lead back to the barn and unharnessed. They each begin to relax as they're given fresh grain and groomed. The odor of their sweaty bodies feels our nostrils and their salty sweat burns the multiple cuts and abrasions on our hands.

We relieve our tired fatigued bodies with splashes of cool creek water. The dried perspiration and prickly hayseed washes swiftly downstream. Oh! What a relief, we are now rejuvenated and ready for a hardy meal.

Our appetites are ravenous, profound and almost unbearable. The aroma of fresh baked cornbread, homemade butter, soup beans, fried potatoes, and fresh brewed coffee fills the air. The aroma only exacerbates the grumbling of our empty stomachs. Each worker takes their assigned seat at the dinner table; grandpa at the "head of the table" the oldest son at the other end of the table, and all other family members are seated on long benches around the table. Every head bows and "The blessing" is given.

The last meal of the day is consumed; dishes are washed, dried, and placed back into the cubbard. Everyone meanders to the front porch, then scurry to his or her favorite chair. We all begin to relax and speak of the day's most embarrassing moments. We poke fun, jokes are made and we all burst out in laughter. The cool summer breeze ruffles our hair, as we begin treating the painful sunburns of those unfortunate ones who decided to remove their shirts while working in the hay field.

As we make plans for the next day's labor, music fills the air, someone's playing a banjo, and our voices harmonize in song. Our bodies are weary, and every muscle aches. Certainly there will be no time for "Tom Foolery" tonight.

# Are there UFOs in Them' There Hills?

Trillions of tiny lights are floating over the fresh mown fields, No! Not UFOs, lightening bugs. The younger kids with jars in-hand are scurrying to-an-fro, and attempting to capture the small gleams of excitement. With treasures in hand, their imaginations are heightened. "Let's make jewelry!" they remove the tails of the lightening bugs; and placing the tails upon their tiny fingers they discover glowing rings, bracelets, and earrings.

I believe the discovery of the UFO was invented by the exhausted imaginations of the city folk. Bored completely out of their gored and feeling the need for a little attention and excitement, they begin to see strange objects in the night sky. Spending most of my life on the farm and the wide open spaces, I never felt the need to create excitement, and certainly was never bored. Therefore, I never witnessed any strange lights in the sky and was never approached or abducted by an alien. However, I've met a lot of strange people in my lifetime.

# Blackberry Picking
## "Watch out for Snakes!"

Its blackberry picking time and the berry vines have produced large sweet juicy fruit. As we start out for the berry field we're warned "Watch out for snakes!" dressed in long sleeve shirts and jeans; of coarse I chose to wear cut-offs and no shoes, "No shoes, you ask?" we wore no shoes in the summer months. New shoes were a luxury that was only afforded during the beginning of a new school year. Besides by mid-summer our bare feet were as tough as shoe leather. Many sewing needles were broken trying to remove the briars that managed to penetrate our bare feet.

We carry multiple 5 gallon pails to the berry field, with the pails strapped to our belts the picking begins. To "Beat the heat of the day" every youngster and the eldest adults work feverishly to fill the buckets as quickly as possible. To keep the youngsters picking and on tract, grandma offers to pay them 5 cents a bucket. Knowing it would take the youngsters all day to pick one bucket, I believe she got a pretty good deal.

Meandering along daydreaming, and filling my berry bucket, I suddenly experience the feeling of what appeared to be the softness of cat tails swirling around my bare legs. I look down toward my feet and see what appear to be a thousand black snakes slithering up my legs and entangling me in their grip. At the top of my lungs I let out a blood curdling scream, "Snakes!!!" this sent everyone heading for higher ground. I dropped that whole bucket of berries and needless to say my picking day was over. That evening as we enjoyed our fresh blackberry cobbler and homemade ice cream the scare of the black snakes was soon forgotten, but will always be remembered.

# Harvest Time
# A Time for Thanks

The lazy days of summer are over; only city-folks call it "Lazy-Days-of-Summer" our lazy days were few-and-far-between. The only "Day of Rest" was Sundays; enjoyed by attending Sunday school and church. After been forgiven of our sins and enjoying fellowship with our neighbors, we return to the farm for our special dinner; fried chicken, fresh vegetables, homemade bread, blackberry cobbler or homemade apple pie. We have this one day to relax and enjoy the things we really like to do.

Our constant praying proved worthy, the harvest is plentiful. Many hours, days, and weeks are spent picking, peeling, shucking, cleaning, cooking, and then preserving our harvest. Once again neighbors join forces, the large canners are readied; jars by the hundreds are washed by hand until their squeaky clean. Wood fires are built, and the copper kettles are readied. Large wooden stirring paddles are brought forth, and the process of making apple butter begins. The hollows and valleys are filled with the scent of apples and cinnamon.

The cellar-house is now packed with hundreds of jars of every vegetable and fruit imaginable. To preserve our bounty of the "Root crop", and affording protection from the deep winter freeze, we dig a huge hole deep into the earth then layer the hole with straw. Ever so gently we place our potatoes, cabbage, carrots, beets, and apples between each layer of straw. A lid made of wooden slabs is then placed over the hole and closed. With our food supply preserved for the winter, our labor intense days are coming to an end, and now is the time to give thanks.

# Autumn
# Cool and Crisp

Cool frosty mornings are nigh. Thick brightly colored patchwork quilts are repaired, and down-filled feather-ticks are stuffed with fresh down. Cords of firewood are chopped and stacked, pumpkins are gathered and their faces carved. In the minds of all young children unexplained bumps and thumps are heard in the night. Ghostly figures appear and then disappear, black cats are amiss, and imaginations run amuck.

We're aware that the shadows are increasing in length, and the hours of daylight are becoming much shorter. The crispness of the wind nips our exposed skin, a reminder that autumn is now here, and the harshness of winter is fast approaching.

Leaves of red, gold, yellow, crimson, and browns are now in their downward spiral. Children work feverishly to mound huge piles of leaves and then propel themselves into the mounds. Sounds of laughter and barking dogs are echoed throughout the holler. As the trees become bare and all plant and animal life begins hibernation, all is silent as the first snowflake falls.

As we begin the early morning ritual of feeding velvety muzzles warm our hands, and we feel the warmth of breathing upon our faces. The bellowing of "Old Brenda" relays a message of urgency; she needs to be relieved of her abundant supply of milk. Rags are warmed and placed around each utter. With the firm and gentle squeezing of my fingers and hands, her warm creamy milk is expelled.

The pinging of the milk splashing against the sides of the tin pail has a rhythmic beat, and eagerly waiting for a few squirts of milk are the "Barn cats". My aim is precise their faces and whiskers are now covered with milk. In the height of their ecstasy the cats quickly clean their faces.

# What's The Big Secret?

Several neighbors gather in one area for butchering day; usually the week of Thanksgiving, and weather permitting As many as 4-6 hogs are butchered and processed in one day. The morning begins very early; large bats of water are heated, and the point of impact is discussed. I'll leave the rest for the imagination.

Processing the meat is very time consuming and extremely tedious. Pounds and pounds of sausage are processed, and the old hand cranked grinder receives a good workout as do the cranker's arm. The carving of the hams and bacon are completed and ready for delivery to the smoke house.

Mr. Smith was the expert at curing hams and bacon, and everyone in the holler took their hams and bacon to his smokehouse to be cured. Mr. Smith was very particular about his smokehouse; he and only he decided who, and if anyone was allowed near his smokehouse. He had one very strict rule; no kids under any circumstances were allowed around or near the smoke house.

I was the most curious of all the kids, so, when I heard his rule I became even more curious. What's the big secret? I waited until everyone was too busy to notice my absence. I slipped-off and out of sight so I thought; I cautiously approached Mr. Smith's smokehouse, slipped around the back of the building, and found a crack between the rough boards. I placed one eye against the crack, and began peeping through. I saw Mr. Smith, and in his right hand he welded a huge knife. He saw me peeping through the crack, and he raised that huge butcher knife and pointed it at me. My God! I was absolutely terrified! I ran from that building as fast as my 8 year old legs would carry me. I need not mention I never, ever returned there again.

# Mincemeat Anyone?

My grandmother made the most delicious mincemeat of anyone in the holler, and she never allowed anyone in the kitchen while she was making the mincemeat. If caught in the kitchen she quickly ordered you out. The aroma of the cinnamon and other spices drifting from her kitchen was too enticing to ignore and again curiosity got the best of me. I had to discover how she made that delicious delicacy. So, I sneaked into the kitchen, and there on top of her stove was a large wash tub. I quickly and quietly pulled up a chair. I climbed onto the chair and peered over the rim of the tub, and to my horror my eyes met two eyes of the hog. I jumped back, tumbled backwards off the chair and landed in the floor with a horrendous crash. My grandmother came running, and with one quick jerk of my arm, she brought me swiftly to my feet. "When will you ever learn to mind your own business?"

There is nothing appetizing or soothing about seeing a hogs head in a wash tub atop a cook stove. I don't give a hoot how good mincemeat smells or tastes; I'll not eat mincemeat again.

# Giving Thanks

Thanksgiving Day is fast approaching and preparation for the Thanksgiving feast begins. It takes several days to prepare a feast for a large family; 20 or more. At least 10 pies of different varieties and at least a dozen loaves of homemade bread are baked. There's stuffing, gravies, puddings, Waldorf salad, and the preparation of the turkey. Oh yes! This is the second purpose for Ole Tom, how very thankful we are for Ole Tom. No more running or carrying a broom to the privy, and no more battles with Ole Tom.

Thanksgiving Day is a very special day for all farmers. Whereby, we all give thanks for the blessings we have received throughout the year; a loving family, lasting friendships, helpful neighbors, a plentiful bounty, and thankful for our good health and the blessing of being protected from all harm; especially men with meat cleavers, wild run away horses, and mean spirited turkeys!

# Fresh Fallen Snow
# The Earth Appears Pure

The freshness of the new fallen snow brings a sense of pureness to the earth. With the approaching harshness of winter our tasks become much more difficult. The livestock must be fed twice daily, and a constant supply of water must be furnished. Water troughs are difficult to maintain when the temperatures' fall and stay below freezing for days on end. Then there's the worry; "Will our feed supply last the entire winter"?

The harsh winter months are difficult for both farmer and his livestock. The farmer must protect his stock from the cold rains and freezing temperatures. During the winter months the farmer spends more time outdoors than in, and his worries are abundant and constant.

However, for the younger kids there are many fun times and precious moments to be remembered; making snow angels, snowball battles, igloos and snowmen to build, and Oh yes! Sleigh rides. The first thing that's needed for a good sleigh ride is about a foot of that pure white stuff.

No brand new shiny sleds were ever purchased from the hardware store, besides, homemade sleds are more functional. Selecting the correct material was crucial; the sled must have the seating capacity of at least 8-10 kids. Want to know the secret? A 12 foot length of used roofing tin; roll-up the front end of the sheet of tin and Waa-la! You have an enormous bob-sled.

Find the largest hill on the farm, load 8-10 kids on the bobsled, and down the hill you go. No steering mechanism needed. If you're headed for a tree or other dangerous object including the livestock, shout "Everyone Off!" No person or animal were ever injured during our fun-filled sleigh rides, only frightened a little.

# "Early to Bed and Early to Rise"

4am comes pretty early no matter where you live. The old adage "Early to Bed and Early to Rise Makes John Healthy Wealthy and Wise" in my book is baloney. First of all; my name is not John, so I think I should've been able to sleep in; but not according to the farm life. The chores had to be completed before catching the school bus at 7am, and then attending school.

Before you've had your breakfast; you dress in layers of clothing, earmuffs, heavy coats, gloves, and knee high boots (no shoes allowed). The mud gets knee deep and there's more than mud in the barnyard; you certainly don't want to loose a shoe or boot in the barnyard. Becoming stuck in the mire and muck is a disaster; the only means out is to grab the tail of a passing cow or horse. With the quick jerk from the animal you usually end up face down in the cold slimy mire.

Heading for the barn and the feeding lot the soft glow of the lantern lights our way. In the darkness you hear the mooing of the cattle, nickering of the horses, bah of the sheep, and squealing of the hogs. Harmonious voices are calling out for their breakfast. Each takes their place in line, side-by-side they patiently wait to be served. Steam emerges from their nostrils and snorts are heard as each buries their muzzle deep into the crisp hay. An overture of smacking and slurping sounds can be heard as the hogs gulp down their warmed slurry of mixed vegetable peels and other materials that grandma decides "Is good for the bacon".

# ADD Disorder Arithmetic?

As teenagers we all began to question authority, and were not easily convinced to believe in our elders' ways. Just as we thought we were mature and began to rebel against their beliefs, we learn the true meaning of "ADD". I'm not speaking of arithmetic. I'm speaking of the medical term Attention Deficit Disorder.

While growing-up there was no such medical term. If by chance the teenager suffered such a disorder, they received treatment immediately. When the elders demanded your attention and you chose to ignore their request; they got your attention, you suffered the deficit, and there certainly would be disorder.

One day I suffered such a disorder; my grandpa and I were weeding the garden. He had just purchased a new gasoline powered garden tiller. Since he and I had always worked the trusty uncomplicated horse, we were a little nervous about operating this contraption. The sound it made was deafening, and Oh my, it smelled bad! My grandpa was a small man 5ft. 9inches, and about 150 pounds. As he pulled the start cord on the contraption, it began moving down the rows of the garden and tossing him about. As he ran over the bean vines he became a little agitated; He yelled something at me. I couldn't hear a word he said, and I made no attempt to try to understand what he had just said, instead I marched passed. The next thing I remembered; I was spitting dirt from my mouth, and picking myself up from the ground. That day I learned the true meaning of "ADD".

# Grandma the Grand Matriarch

With hay mowed and stacked, and the gardens planted we now had time for mischief and fun; Time for swimming, horse back riding, spending the night with friends, playing in the creek, and catching crawl dads. These fun times allowed me time to develop many precious memories, and from those precious memories developed some funny stories.

Before marrying my grandpa my grandma was a school teacher; teaching grades 7 through 8. I believe her teaching experience gave her the ability to handle all types of ornery kids. There was absolutely no way of outsmarting her.

She was a large framed lady; 5ft. 11 inches, and weighing about 160lbs. with exceptionally long legs, and could run as fast as a thoroughbred. The only way we could out run her was to get a good head start. No matter how big or smart we thought we were; she had a solution for every shenanigan we tried to pull.

She was mighty wicked with a broom, and an excellent marksman. She was the most respected, feared and loved by all the family, the "Grand Matriarch".

# Mischievous Boy
# Tiger's Missing Tail

We had discovered a new humane way of removing lamb's tails, much better than cutting off then burning the stub. We called it tail bands; I really didn't know the proper name, but the process was amazing. You place the band similar to a rubber band around each lamb's tail. The process took several weeks for the tail to drop. The lambs suffered no pain; it sealed off the incision and protected the lambs' rear end from infection.

One of my mischievous cousins's decided he would try one of the bands on my grandma's most precious cat, Tiger. Several weeks passed and then it happened. I heard grandma yelling, "Jimmy! Jimmy! Something's wrong with my Tiger cat!" We all ran outside, and sure enough Tiger was swaying to-and-fro up the driveway. He was off balance and his tail was gone.

We all began laughing, but it was no laughing matter for grandma. Immediately grabbing her broom and missing no part of his body, she began swatting Jimmy.

How did she know he was the culprit? It took several days for Tiger to regain his balance; he survived the ordeal and wobbled along without his tail for many years thereafter.

# The Silver Maple Tree
# Grandma the Great Marksman

On our farm we had a grand old Silver Maple tree that stood by the old farm house, like everything on the farm it too had a purpose; it was made for climbing.

As teenagers we were approaching the time in our lives whereby we all became a little rebellious; we thought we were much smarter, stronger, could out run, and climb trees much faster than our adult counterparts.

Whenever grandma gave us chores that we thought were unfair, or should've been dealt to someone our junior, our rebellion began. Being disrespectful and out of reach of a "backhand" or broom, we'd begin to protest by raising our voices. In the 50's and early 60's "back talk" was absolutely not allowed, and you best not even have the facial expression of using profanity because lye soap in the mouth is worse than drinking Drain-O.

Jimmy was two years my senior and therefore, my mentor. I watched and learned how he used the tree to try and out fox grandma. Jimmy was the first to give the 50 foot Maple tree its purpose; he averaged climbing that tree at least once a week.

The morning started early and the chores were assigned. Jimmy began his protest, "That's not my job its Jeanie's, and you can just make her do it!" Grandma; "You best shut your mouth and do what I say!" Jimmy; "And if I don't whatcht'ya gonna do!?" Grandma; "I'll show you!" as Jimmy darted for the tree, grandma headed for the rock filled driveway. We would soon learn that grandma was the greatest marksman that ever lived. She could hit the bull's-eye of any target 100 yards away; her ammo—rocks. I swear I don't believe she ever used that apron for cooking, but for the purpose of carrying her ammo.

Holding the apron with one hand and using the other to fill her apron with rocks, she returned to the tree and began pelting Jimmy with the rocks. Striking her target with each blow the great marksman began yelling, "You best come down or I'll knock you down!" Forget the "Red Rider BB gun", and "Shooting your eye out". I truly believed that if Jimmy had not come down, he would've been killed, or a least suffer several broken bones from the fall. After the second or third shot fired by the great marksman, Jimmy decided it would be much safer to be beaten by the broom than being killed by the rock hurling grandma.

# A New Plan atop the Roof
# The Great Whopper

I observed Jimmy for several weeks continually being defeated. So, I devised a plan to avoid the broom, and the rock hurling grandma. If I could get a head start I could climb the tree and cross over onto the roof of the farm house. The ridge of the roof would afford me protection from the great marksman and her rocks. Feeling more confident and rebellious I decided that today is a perfect day to refuse to clean out the chicken house; besides its 90 degrees out and the chickens were smelly and dirty. I announced that "I didn't think I should have to do that, that's a boy's job!" Grandma calmly stated "That's your job for the summer, why do you think it should be a boy's job?" Me; "because I don't want to do it." Grandma: "Well guess what? You're going to do it." Me; "Well I guess not". She reached for the broom; I was expecting this one. I took off like a streak of lightening with her swatting me all the way to the tree. Grasping the tree limbs one by one up I went. About eight feet up the tree I was now out of her reach; she turned and headed for the driveway.

As she was busy filling her apron with rocks I jumped from the tree to the roof top, and I began laughing; HA! HA! HA! Boy am I clever or what. I headed to the ridge of the roof; she returned with her ammo, and began hurling the rocks up and over the roof top. Dodging the hurling rocks I hung onto the roofs ridge, straddled it and immediately lay down and swung to the opposite side of the roof. Now with the protection of the roofs ridge the only target she had was my tiny head.

I had the upper hand; I could see her there on the ground and knew her every move. As she started to make her move to the other side of the house where I was lying; I'd straddle the roofs ridge and swing to the opposite side of the roof. She continued to throw rocks; she'd throw a rock, I'd duck, she'd throw another I'd duck. After several attempts of her hurling rocks at me and missing her target, she gave up and went back inside the house. My well thought out plan actually worked, and I came out unscaved. I was more than ready to get off that roof. Jeepers it sure was hot up there, must have been at least 150 degrees on that tin roof.

Before I could come down from the roof I had to make sure the coast was clear. I walked all four corners of the roof several times, looking down at the ground making sure she Was nowhere in sight. With the coast clear it was safe to come down. I cautiously climbed off the roof and back into the tree and down to the ground. Believing I had out foxed her, I made my way around the house to the kitchen door. I cupped my two hands together and peered through the screen door. There she was, in the kitchen doing her ironing as I had hoped.

"Are you thirsty?" "Yes". "Well, come on in and get a drink". I sheepishly opened the screen door, and walked to the water bucket. Just as I picked up the ladle to get a well deserved drink, that darn broom reappeared, and on my behind I felt a Whop! Whop! Whop! Grandma could get off more whops than an automatic rifle with that broom.

I'm much older now, and as I reminisce; a smile comes to my

lips. I never out-smarted her, she heard my every footstep on that old tin roof, and knew exactly when I came off the roof; and she was prepared to give me a well deserved whopping.

# A Frightening Car Ride
# The End of the World

We lived 35 miles from the nearest town; therefore, going to town was a grand event. Being from a large family not everyone could go at once, it would be months before you were chosen; providing you were a good little boy or girl and done all that was asked of you.

The Saturday I was chosen to go with my grandpa and grandma was a very exciting day. Doing extra chores I had earned 25 cents; I know 25 cents doesn't sound like much today, back then it was a fortune for a young child. I could buy; 5-candy bars, 5-oatmeal cakes, a movie ticket, or 5-bottles of soda pop.

As we drove along the winding road towards the main town I was dreaming of what I could buy with all that money; when all of a sudden the sky became as black as night. Bracing herself with both hands atop the cars ceiling my grandma began yelling "Oh! Pa the world is coming to an end!"

Now, my grandpa being a minister we had heard about the time when the world would come to an end. Believing everything my grandparents' had taught me, my cousin and I dove for the floorboard of the car and covered our heads. What this would do to save us I had no idea. All I knew was… that in an atomic bomb attack our teachers had taught us to lie down and cover our heads.

My grandpa pulled the car to the side of the road, and the only sound heard in the darkness was the humming of the cars engine; neither grandpa nor grandma uttered a single word; in a child's mind this made the situation even more frightening. All was silent as we waited for the "End of Time", and the unknown.

It seemed like an eternity before the sun slowly began to reappear, and my grandparents gave no explanation as to what had just happened. It was not until a couple years later while attending the 6$^{th}$ grade that I learned the mystery; it was an eclipse.

# The Good Sheppard

On our farm we raised sheep, sheared them for their wool and sold it for hopefully a profit. I really didn't care for the older sheep, but I sure loved the lambs. Every spring there was always a ewe that would either reject her lambs, or unfortunately die giving birth. Sounds selfish, but with each lambing season I always hoped that one or two of the lambs would be orphaned, this would allow me the privilege to bottle raise the orphans, and maybe keep them as pets. Very seldom were we ever allowed to keep pets on the farm; they were too costly to keep, and could serve no purpose.

As luck would have it the lambing season came and I was awarded two tiny lambs to bottle raise, I proudly named them; Bucky and Susie. Knowing that I would not be allowed to keep them as pets, I spent every moment possible with them, thoroughly enjoying the times we romped and cuddled.

It was getting close to the time when they would be taken to market. So, my sister and I came up with a plan; we would hide the lambs. They would not be found until the stock truck was on its way to the stock sale.

My mother and dad were having an addition added onto our house, my sister and I decided we would hide Bucky and Susie between unfinished walls of the addition. We would place the lambs there for safe keeping.

Evening came and the lambs were no where to be found. Grandma became extremely worried, she notified my uncle and everyone else on the farm; there's two lambs missing! Not knowing that all good Sheppard's count their flocks nightly; I couldn't understand how on earth she knew there were two measly lambs missing… after all she had sixty-three head, and each of those had at least two babies. They counted and recounted the flock; still there were two missing.

They called my dad and asked if he had seen the lambs; overhearing the conversation, and not being asked, my sister and I kept quite. As darkness approached the tiny critters began calling out for their evening bottle. Their cries directed my mother to their location, she found the tiny creatures between the walls addition and notified my grandma. In a very stern voice she instructed my sister and I "You return those lambs immediately!" We retrieved the lambs from the wall and returned them to our grandmother.

My grandma wasn't upset that we had hid the lambs; my grandma always had a gentle and kind way of explaining things to her grandchildren. A way that we could understand and then explain what the right thing was to do in all situations.

I truly believed she knew exactly how we felt. She asked "why on earth did you hide the lambs?" I explained that we loved them so much that we didn't want them to go to market. She stated "God gave us these little lambs so we can make a decent living on the farm, besides they'll help pay for new shoes and clothes; Christmas is coming, and we'll need the extra cash". Well then, since Christmas is coming and we need extra money, it'll be ok to send them to market. There would be many more times that I would be chosen to bottle raise the orphaned lambs.

# Oh! Christmas Tree,
# Oh! Christmas tree

As young children we all looked forward to Christmas, and having the grandest Christmas tree ever, my bothers, sisters and I were no exception. When we were younger my dad was the one who always retrieved our tree. My brothers and I decided this year we would help our dad out and find that perfect tree.

Now, pine trees were less than abundant where we lived, therefore we had to begin our search weeks in advance, and would need to travel several miles to find the perfect tree. Without money to purchase a tree, we decided the tree must be one that no one would care if we took.

Riding the school bus every morning and afternoon gave us the perfect opportunity to survey nearby farms. Each day as we road along we searched diligently, and finally we spotted the perfect tree. Standing alone by its self on the hillside of a nearby farm, we were sure that it was the tree that no one would want. My brothers and I were thrilled and began making plans to fetch the tree that evening.

Darkness was fast approaching as my brothers and I began our preparation to fetch the tree; as we were pulling our homemade sled from the shed, we were interrupted by my large white collie Rowdy; announcing loudly to everyone within ear shot that he wanted to tag along. He could not be allowed to tag along on this trip. I immediately ordered him to lie down, be quiet and stay! With his head and ears lowered, and his pouty face he obeyed the command; So, I thought.

Pulling the sled behind us we started the two mile hike to retrieve the tree. As we reached the farm it was now pitch dark, but we knew the exact location of the tree. With the ax in hand we began chopping, after several whacks the tree was down. Oh, how proud we were, it was a magnificence tree. We towed the tree back to the house and began decorating. It was the most beautiful tree we had ever had; better than the ones my dad had ever gotten.

My dad returned from work and asked "Where did you all get that tree"? We explained that we had found it on a farm not far from where we lived. He asked "Did you get permission to take the tree?" We explained that we took one that we thought no one would want. He announced in a much sterner voice "That's not what I asked; I asked did you get permission to take the tree?" We each lowered our heads and replied "No". He stated "I know exactly where you got the tree, Mr. Lloyd saw Rowdy following you along the hillside and he knew it was our dog. You will pay Mr. Lloyd for the tree."

My dad explained that this was stealing, and our family is not ones to be known as thieves. Needless to say we each received our due punishment that evening, we sang out in harmony, but for some reason it sure didn't sound anything like "Oh Christmas tree-Oh Christmas tree".

# Yes Jeanie, there is a Santa Claus Just not Red Hair

Christmas was fast approaching, and the excitement was unbearable. The weeks flew by as we attended school and church plays, our Christmas spirit was soaring. We could hardly wait for Christmas. As all children we made our Christmas wishes known as we viewed the pages of the Christmas edition of the Sears & Roebuck catalog.

In the hollow where I grew-up Santa made rounds to each house in the hollow on Christmas Eve, and while eagerly awaiting his arrival we all kept a vigilant eye out for Ole Santa. This Christmas would be one I would never forget, discovering that Santa was someone other than himself, was the most traumatic one I'd ever experienced.

It was a perfect Christmas Eve and a beautiful night for a visit from Santa; the sky was clear, the moon was as bright as daylight, and the ground was covered with a skiff of fresh glistening snow; Santa's reindeer would have no trouble seeing their way or towing his sleigh to our house tonight. As we eagerly awaited his arrival, I could hear my older brother and sisters whispering, and by their whispering conversation, I came to the conclusion that they no longer believed in Santa. "Who do you think he is?" they mentioned several names in their whisperings, but I tried to pay no mind as to what they were discussing.

The moonlight allowed us a clear view to the end of the

hollow; therefore we could see Santa's every move. We saw him cross the bridge to our cousin's house, and then to my grandpa's. Our excitement became more intense as he was now making his way slowly toward our house.

He was only minutes away! Seconds away, and now approaching our very own driveway! He had now reached the top of the hill to our driveway! He took one step in the attempt to descend the steep driveway. Then suddenly he slipped and began tumbling head-over-heels down the steep hillside; his magical black toy sack flew through the air, loosing all its contents. We stood there in complete disbelief, and horror as Santa continued to tumble out of control. My mother and dad began laughing. How horrible I thought they were; this was no laughing matter, Santa was about to be killed!

Santa ended his journey at the bottom of the fifty foot driveway; Still dizzy from all the tumbling, he stood up his suit was now in complete disarray; his snow white beard was cocked sideways; entangled with sticks, leaves, and mud, giving the appearance of a dirty brown beard. His hat was cocked to one side of his head, and protruding from his head was a huge mass of uncontrolled Flaming Red Hair! My oldest brother yelled out the most horrible revelation I had ever heard; "Oh My God! Its Homer and he's drunk!" My younger brothers and I were totally traumatized, and began loudly sobbing. We were horrified, thinking that Homer was Santa and he was drunk. What a traumatic experience for a six, seven and eight year old; probably the most traumatic experience we would ever experience in a life time.

My mother and dad rushed to Santa's side and began

reassuring us that Homer was only filling-in for Santa and he was not drunk. The real Santa would visit tonight after we were all fast asleep. We were then rushed off to bed, again being reassured that Santa would visit us after we were fast asleep.

Still traumatized by the evenings event, I asked my dad later if Santa was real, his response "Yes Jeanie, there is a real Santa Claus". I can't speak for my younger brothers, but I slept surprisingly well that night and had no terrifying dreams. We awoke that morning with great excitement; the real Santa had made his visit during the night after we were all fast asleep.

# The Greatest Surprise

My love for horses began when I was about 3-4 years old. My uncle above all my family understood my obsession for horses. He was the most instrumental in teaching me all he knew about horses, and he knew a lot. Before I was of school age he would take me with him when he "worked the horses". There was Nell, Silver, Flicka, and Pearl; later came Fred, Fancy, and Duke. Our group was sisters, brothers, mothers and daughters. Our colts came out of the sire "Wheeler" a huge sorrel Belgian, with flaxen mane and tail.

My mother was extremely frightened of horses, but that didn't affect me one bit. At the age of four I had no fear; in fact when my uncle would leave the horses in the field and go to the house for lunch, off to the field I'd go to be with the horses. I would stack rocks as high as I needed too, to reach the first rung of the harness. Then just like a little monkey, I'd climb up the harness until I reached the horses back. I would sit there until my uncle returned to the field. He had no objections; he knew that Flicka was the most trusting horse on the farm, and I was quite safe atop her huge frame "A Gentle Giant".

One day I heard my mother calling me. I ignored her calls as I sat there like a queen on the back of Flicka. Knowing she was petrified of horses, I was safe from her grasp; after all she wouldn't come near Flicka. She saw me sitting on top of this huge 1000 pound beast, and began yelling, "Jeanie you get down from there you'll be killed!" As she kept a safe distance, I continued to reassure her not to worry that I was quite safe. My uncle returned to the field and calmly instructed "Jeanie, you best come down, you've scared your mother to death, she just doesn't understand." To this day my mother still talks about the great surprise she got that day; seeing me atop that huge beast, and not knowing how on earth such a small child could reach the top of that beast.

# No Baby Dolls Please
# Selfish Attitude

As most young girls I dreamed of having a pony of my own. I was obsessed with horses, day and night I talked about horses. My brothers and sisters poked constant fun at me; I drove my mother and dad insane; constantly nagging for a pony.

I watched every western that our old black and white Zenith TV could receive on our make shift antenna; I really didn't care about the theme of the story, I just wanted to see the horses; the Lone Ranger and Silver, Roy Rogers and Trigger, Dale Evans and Buttermilk, My Friend Flicka, and Fury; complete obsession.

It was my birthday and I was sure I would receive a pony. My mother baked me a beautiful birthday cake, and atop were 8 candles. My family sang "Happy Birthday to you….." I blew out the candles and made my wish; really no need to make a wish, everyone was quite aware of what my wish was.

I opened my brothers and sisters presents first; pictures of different breeds of horses placed on wooden plaques to hang in my room. As I thanked each and everyone for their gifts, I began to believe that my wish was about to come true; since they had given me these beautiful pictures of all types of horses; it must be a prelude to me receiving my dream.

My mother entered the room with a huge beautifully wrapped box, thinking to myself; this wasn't a pony… but maybe it's outside. With a smile my mother said "open it Jeanie, I hope you like it." I slowly opened the package; it wasn't a pony, but a plastic doll! "I don't like it, it stinks!" She didn't smell like a horse, she smelled like the awful smell of plastic. I saw the hurt on my mother's face as I made the ungrateful remark. I apologized for my actions, and began playing with the doll, but she knew I was disappointed. I was even more disappointed with myself. I knew my mother paid a lot for that doll, and spent money that we probably didn't have. I wondered how she could ever forgive me.

How could I show her that I truly appreciate all that she does? I decided… from that day forward I would be at my mothers side, helping her in ever way I could; carrying water for the washing, hanging out the wash, anything she asked me to do. I would be at her beckon call, and decided that I would make her birthdays special as she had tried for me. That next year I did just that.

With the resources I had available I made every attempt to make her birthday as special as an 8 year old could. I constructed a birthday card from freezer paper, and with crayon, inscribed a loving birthday message. Having no scotch tape, and using black electrical tape, I attached a bouquet of wildflowers and roses from her garden on the front; not real attractive, but she said it was a beautiful card. I bake a birthday cake covered with creamed icing; the first cake I'd ever baked.

I can't remember if the cake and card were all that beautiful, but she told me they were. From that day forward I tried to do everything possible to please my mother. As time passed I realized that she had forgiven me for the ungratefulness I had displayed that August.

# The Pony I truly did not deserve

It was a crisp November evening, and I had no clue as what was about to transpire. I saw the lights of a large truck slowly coming up our dirt road; I could hear the neighing of what appeared to be ponies. My dad met the truck at the end of the driveway. He spoke to the man for a short time, and then called for me to join them. My brothers, sisters and I ran to the truck. There inside were several young ponies, different colors and sizes. As we peered through the slats on the trucks bed, my dad announced "Jeanie which one do you want." I was absolutely speechless; it took me several minutes before it registered what he had just said. With my dad shining a flashlight through the slats, I saw the most beautiful pony I had ever laid eyes on; a sorrel, with white mane and tail, a silver muzzle, and silver legs. A mix between; Trigger and My Friend Flicka; The pony came over to where I was standing, and placed his warm muzzle against my hand. I eagerly announced; this is the one, "I want him!" The seller said "his name is J&M King, he's a registered Shetland pony, came from Sheppard's Town WV, he's a stallion, and will make you a fine pony".

We unloaded King and took him to the barn, whereby, I immediately placed fresh straw in his stall, gave him fresh water and grain, then began grooming him. I stayed with him that night as long as my mother would allow; after all I had school the next day. Boy! Did I ever have a big announcement to make at school the next day.

As I stood there grooming King, the thought of my behavior the previous August, brought me to tears. How could I have been so hurtful to my mother? She now had rewarded me with another very special gift. A gift that I felt I truly did not deserve. I realized at that moment that my mother had forgiven me, and in turn I could now forgive myself.

As I look back on those days; I learned a very valuable lesson; I would never be that ungrateful again, and would teach my own children not to be selfish or ungrateful. Always think of others, take nothing for granted, and be very grateful for what they are given.

# The Great White Hunters

Daniel Boone was my brothers hero; his ability to track and trap wild animals, and the many dangerous adventures in which he partook, was captivating, and had a great impact on many young boys, especially my brother. According to my brother's standard Daniel Boone was the greatest hunter and scout that ever lived. My brother more-so than me, wanted to be "just like Daniel Boone".

My brother had a way of making his well thought out adventures sound so logical and always had a way of convincing me to come along. He came up with a plan to go "groundhog hunting". He had been scouting out a groundhogs burrow for several days; His plan was to catch her and her babies, then we could sell the babies and make some extra money. Now, there's nothing cuter than a baby groundhog, so it didn't take much to convince me to partake in the adventure.

He assured me that he knew exactly how to catch her; his plan was to get a burlap sack, place it over the entrance hole of the groundhogs burrow; set a rag on fire and smoke her out from the other end of the burrow. I was to hold the burlap sack over the entrance hole; as she exited the hole and entered the sack, I was to close and tie the sack.

I got down on my knees in front of the burrow and placed the sack over the hole as my brother had instructed. As he set the rag on fire it released a huge cloud of smoke. He stuck the smoking rag into the burrow and yelled "Get ready, she's coming out!" He was absolutely right she darted out of the burrow and plunged into the burlap sack knocking me backwards. With the groundhog inside I was now wrestling the sack and the groundhog, and making ever attempt to tie the sack. Finally with the sack tied the groundhog was now safe and secure.

Our prize captured, and our mission accomplished; I felt "just like Daniel Boone". As I attempted to carry the hog with an outstretched arm I realized she was too heavy. I decided I'd carry her over my shoulder. I swung the burlap sack over my right shoulder allowing it to rest on my back. As the sack hit my back I felt as though I'd been struck by lightening. "Holy! Moley!" The groundhog had sunk her razor sharp teeth into my right shoulder. I let out a war whoop and swung that sack around as though I was playing for a major league baseball team; the groundhog and sack were now airborne; separating the groundhog from the sack she was now airborne; first time I ever saw a flying groundhog.

As she landed and scampered past my brother then disappeared, he began yelling at me; "I can't believe you let her get away!" I explained what had just happened. He lifted the back of my shirt and there in plain view was the proof. I had a huge set of upper and lower teeth marks on my right shoulder, didn't draw blood or break the skin but it sure was painful.

The great white hunters had many more death defying adventures and lived to tell the story of each and every one.

# The Great Fox Hunter's Friday Night Survival

Fox hunters always have a pack of hounds; consisting of about 3-6 hounds each, my dad and grandpa were no exception. They were great fox hunters; and every Friday night after working in town they'd come home, have their dinner then announce that we kids were to help them get the dogs ready for the chase. We dreaded Friday nights; the punishment we had to endure was unbelievable.

My dad had 6 hounds and my grandpa had four to six; for a total of about 10-12 dogs and weighing about 45 pounds each. Now, getting this many dogs ready to do what they absolutely loved to do turns out to be one of the most chaotic scenarios that one could ever witness, and probably the most hilarious.

The hounds develop a learned behavior; it's been five days since they were attached to collars and lead straps then hauled to the woods and turned loose. Their goal; to find a fox give chase, and hopefully for the fox hunters delight the chase would continue throughout the entire night.

The trucks are backed near the dog pins, and at this point the hounds know exactly what's about to transpire. The hounds are collared, connected to their lead straps, and the gate is opened.

Every attempt is made to lead the excited uncontrollable dogs to the waiting trucks, and in the blink of an eye the people and dogs become absolutely and completely out of control.

10 to 12-45 pound dogs are now barking and jumping higher than our heads, 6-8 people are yelling at the top of their lungs, hounds are jerking and knocking us kids to the ground; entangling the adults in the lead straps. We all end up in a huge mangled pile of human bodies and dogs. With heads, arms, legs and tails protruding from the mangled pile; the event resembles a world wide wrestling event, and the possibility of being injured is strong, but luck has it, no one or a single dog is ever injured.

Everyone regroups and begins loading the hounds into the trucks, and the situation becomes less chaotic, but the noise continues to be deafening. The trucks are now headed out of the hollow. As their distance of travel becomes further and further from the house, there's a sigh of relief, another Friday night survived.

# Lets Play Tag
# "The Cow's it"

Living on the farm and having to travel many miles to be entertained was an impossibility. Therefore, we had to develop ways of entertaining ourselves and each other. We were able to come up with some pretty ingenuous ways of entertaining ourselves. My favorite was playing tag in the dark; there were no available flashlights, so we played in pitch-darkness.

This game of tag could be somewhat dangerous; in the darkness of the night the plan is too seek out and find someone to tag then yell "you're it!" Now, running at break-neck speed in pure darkness is totally insane and down right dangerous.

The only way you could find a person to tag was to use your six senses; forget the eyesight; nothing to see, after all its pitch dark. The use of smell was somewhat helpful; especially if the person hadn't had a bath in a while. Taste; well if you stumbled and fell face down in what ever you'd end up tasting something. Hearing was the most helpful; you could hear footsteps, giggling, and feel the brief puff of air as the person rushes passed you.

As you play the game you're running blindly through the dark, listening intensely and hoping to tag a person; and having no thought of tagging an 800 pound cow.

I was "it" I could hear the kids giggling and felt poufs of air as they passed by me. In hot pursuit and with outstretched arms I tagged no one. I then heard a couple of kid's crash into one another. As they hit the ground with a thud; I believed this was my opportunity to tag someone. I began running at break-neck speed to where I thought they had landed.

At the same time my brother yells "Holy Moley the cows are out!" my entire body struck something huge and soft. With a loud thud I sprang off the cow's stomach, bounced backwards and hit the ground. I yelled "I just tagged the cow, she's it". Everyone burst out in a belly-rolling laughter.

# Mowing the Lawn Not with the Butt

Many backbreaking and intense hours were spent mowing our acre lawn with a push type mower. The old push style lawn mower measured about 2 feet in width; and had two steel wheels, a long wooden handle; and at the end of the handle was a T that formed the handle grips, allowing the pusher to grip and push the mower. It had four rotary blades that were connected to the axle, when the mower was pushed the wheels turned, thus turning the blades and cutting the grass.

My brother; next to the youngest of three, was the most ingenious of all. He informed my cousin and me that he had read that there was a contraption on the market called a riding lawn mower. Stating that he had not seen its picture, but it's supposed to make mowing a lawn much easier and faster.

He could only imagine how a riding mower would operate; he explained to my cousin and me that if he could sit on the handle of the push mower and ride it down the hill, mowing the hill would be much faster and therefore we wouldn't have to push it up and down the hill to mow. This made perfect sense and sounded logical.

He took the mower to the top of the hill sat his butt down on the wooden handle of the mower, and placed his feet on the safety guard over the blades. He then instructed my cousin and me to shove him down the steep hill. We did just as he had instructed.

As he was sailing down the hill and yelling "Yee Haw!" the mower was mowing the grass just as he had predicted. Just as he was nearing the bottom of the hill his feet slipped off the blade guard, throwing his butt cheeks onto the rotary blades. Rolling off the mower he began yelling "Holy Cow, Holy Cow!" I just cut off half my butt!" As he stood and turned around his torn blood soaked britches was definitely proof that he had cut off a huge chunk of his butt. Cupping both his butt cheeks in his hands we made our way back to the house.

How could we conjure up a believable story, and how this happened? We decided there was no way we could ever come up with a believable story, so we decided it would be best if we just tell the truth; after all, no one not even my dad would spank my brother's injured butt.

# Blind as a Mule

Before we were able to build up our teams of horses we would on certain occasions have to borrow a team from a neighbor; especially in the spring when our two mares were about to foal and our "mama's to be" could not be allowed to pull the heavy farm equipment.

Having good neighbors my uncle had no problem borrowing a single horse or a team if need be. This particular Saturday my uncle needed a single horse to pull a sled full of manure; his plan was to spread the manure in one of our orchards. He spoke with several nearby farmers and the only beast available this Saturday, was a mule named Bill; a large black and brown Missouri mule standing about 16 hands.

My uncle was quite familiar with horses, but had no experience working mules; He explained to me that there's not much difference in horses and mules; but I had always heard that mules were quite stubborn and much more difficult to work.

Saturday morning arrived and in the meadow below our farmhouse I saw my uncle and Bill making their way slowly towards our farmhouse towing a large manure filled sled. I quickly dressed and ran to meet them.

My uncle announced that he would need me to ride Bill so that he could ride the sled and throw the manure. He had only one set of instructions; "Make all your turns Haul (left), Bill doesn't go Gee" (right). I asked why, he stated "Just keep his turns left". He boosted me atop that large beast and away we went. After riding Bill about a quarter mile and feeling more confident; I decided that my uncle was absolutely right; there wasn't much difference in horses and mules.

We spent several hours spreading the manure; as instructed I always guided Bill in straight lines, and at the end of each row would turn him left. As we were making the last row of spreading the manure, Bill decided enough was enough; he began heading straight for an apple tree. As we were coming closer and closer to the tree I made every attempt to turn him left, he absolutely refused to turn left. I pulled with all my strength and he would not heed. He decided he was turning right and did just that.

He lowered his head; too late for me to duck the branches, and he dragged me through the tree. As I emerged from the tree Bill stopped dead in his tracks; saving my uncle from the torture I had just received. My face, neck and arms were now burning from the scratches received from the branches. My uncle began laughing, asking "are you all right? I told you to keep him going left".

I saw nothing funny about the situation and sternly asked "why will he not turn Gee?" He stated "Oh, I forgot to tell you, he's blind in his right eye." "It's a fine time to tell me now!" I still believe that blind stubborn mule had every intention of dragging me off. The fact he was blind had nothing to do with him heading straight for that tree, and his refusal to turn left when commanded confirmed my suspiousions; he sure could turn right when it was convenient for him.

# With Each New Season
# There's Also Conclusion

I'm much older now, and as I reminisce I have so many fond memories of my growing up on the farm. We shared a deep abiding love for God, our families, neighbors, and our country. Our friends were true friends, our neighbors were true neighbors. We were always there for one another, and we shared every experience in the worst of times and the best.

Farm living moves at a much slower pace, allowing the farmer and his family the luxury of enjoying what they are given, and to share the extra they are able to produce. This way of life is slowly being lost by the greed and fast pace in which we are living. We all need to learn to slow down and do with a little less, spend quality time with our families, and enjoy what we have. You may come to realize that living with a little less is not so bad; that a peaceful heart, healthy body and mind is worth more than monetary value.

We need to slow down and realize that with every season there comes conclusion; whether it be a wedding, the birth of a child or grandchild, the death of a loved one, or the loss of income, we shall all survive with the love of God, family, and friends.

I wish you all well, and hope you've enjoyed this book.